Critter Riddles And Rhymes

Critter Riddles And Rhymes

By

Mark H. Glissmeyer

Gradina Books

Copyright © 2022 by Mark H. Glissmeyer

All rights reserved.

No part of this book may be reproduced, or stored in a retrieval system, or transmitted in any form or by any means, electronic, mechanical, recording, photocopying, or otherwise, without the express written consent of the publisher.

ISBN-13: 978-0-9985416-9-3

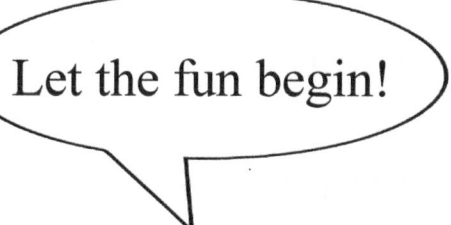

Caution:

Sharks just want to be friends
they say to make some amends.
So that's what we hear
but I won't swim near
to find out what one intends.

Question:

Can critters have a good laugh,
if one of them has a bad gaffe?
Some research says yes,
it's what they possess.
Just watch as they double in half.

Noises:

Why is there always a crow
that has to let everyone know
it is a riot
by not keeping quiet,
then flies away terribly slow?

Coincidences:

Beavers will always love to gnaw.
Their dream is to own a chainsaw.

Riddle:

I was born with a nose
that's long like a hose.
It'll even shoot far
and wash any car.
What critter am I?

Odors:

There once was a young baby skunk
who hid in the skirt of a monk.
As he walked in the mission
there was no beautician,
so everyone winced as he stunk.

Question:

Are you really a fowl,
and why have that scowl?

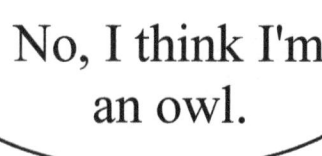

Squawkers:

Two rabbits once heard a squawk
when above them flew by a hawk.
If that meant distress
they'd never confess
since that was the last time they'd talk.

Oddity:

A large bear once tried to bark
while inside a national park,
and it appeared quite weird,
like a man with a beard,
so they shipped him off to Denmark.

Riddle:

While underwater I'll swim
without using a limb.
I'm not the quickest,
but my skin is the thickest.
What critter am I?

Refreshments:

Iguanas do whatever they wanna
when outside it's hot as a sauna,
like doing push-ups
while drinking in cups
of tequila when in Tijuana.

Caution:

Be careful around a mosquito
that's slender like a taquito,
since it bites in your skin
and gets a big grin
as you bloat up like a burrito.

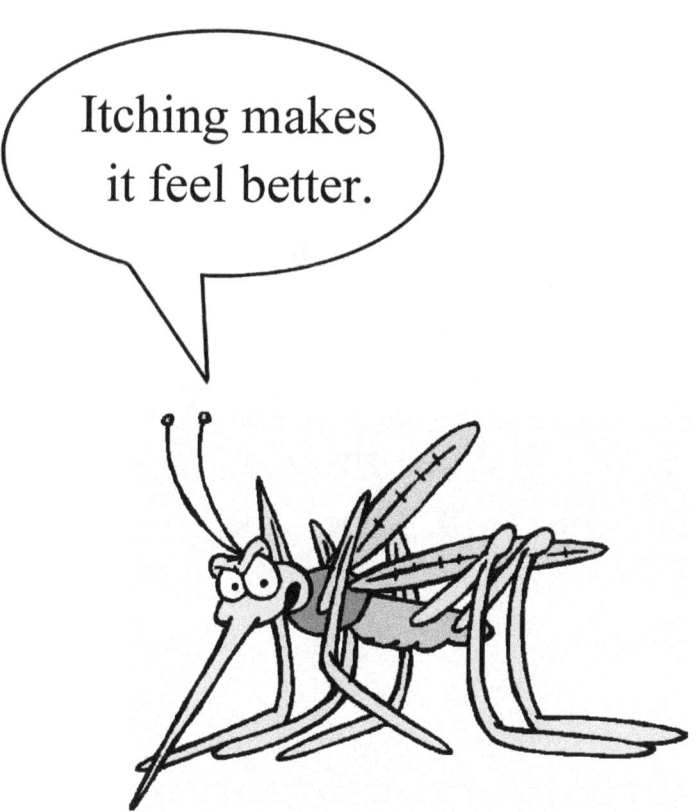

Laughs:

Hyenas know how to laugh
and can moo just like a calf,
but when confronted by fear
you'll just see their rear
as they run with their tails tucked in half.

Funnies:

Everyone smiles at a monkey
from dropouts to even a flunky,
but when in a zoo
they like to throw doo.
Try not to get hit when it's chunky.

Warning:

If you ever see a big spider
open its mouth up much wider,
don't ask for an "Aah"
or pull at its claw,
you just might end up inside her.

Please play with me, I'm hungry.

Crazies:

Think of the small tiny worm
for digging can't be too firm,
but some think they're neat
to cook for a treat,
leaving others to wiggle and squirm.

Riddle:

I can always outlast
and none are this fast
while running with spots
much larger than dots.
What critter am I?

Fibbers:

There once was a funny grasshopper
who fibbed and told a big whopper.
It claimed to ride fast
without being asked
while going full speed on a chopper.

Relaxers:

Who would believe that a rhino
loved to hear music that I know.
Until came a sound
that made its heart pound,
and now it drinks like a wino.

Magicians:

Chameleons will often change colors
so they don't look like their brothers.
But they also can switch.
So which one is which?
It even confuses their mothers.

Riddle:

I am known as the highest
even where it's the driest,
and can nibble on trees
without bending my knees.
What critter am I?

Not fair, you peeked at me....

Munchers:

There once was a possum
that ate the wrong blossom,
which made its head spin
like it swallowed some gin,
and now it feels so awesome.
.

Hiders:

Polar Bear figures are low
they say due to melting snow.
But given more years,
there's more than appears.
So how do we all really know?

Warning:

Nothing can rhyme with a zebra,
not even a tiny amoeba.

Swimmers:

While catching a lobster by the tail
a diver was swallowed by a whale,
but then it had doubt,
so spit him right out,
and spouted off just like a quail.

Question:

I could be dancing
and I should be prancing,
without wearing a sock
as I do the moonwalk.
Who do I like imitating?

Forests:

A small fox once walked by a tree
until it was hard to see.
There's nothing to explain
why it's yellow like rain
since a koala was taking a wee.

Caution:

Nobody likes seeing a nose
getting picked just like a rose.
But it has to begin
when ants crawl in,
since nothing works better I suppose.

Question:

Have you ever seen a big cat
play golf while wearing a hat?
It may seem too formal
and act quite abnormal,
so don't ever try to chitchat.

Riddle:

I may seem very slow
and barely walk as I go,
with a shell on my back
that prevents an attack.
What critter am I?

Traditions:

A duck became quite outspoken
on how its leg became broken.
But to make it get better,
it got wrapped in a sweater,
and used some bath salts to soak in.

Sleepers:

There once was a tiny small snake
that hid and slept in a cake.
When they served a small slice
a guest paid the price
and awoke with a big belly ache.

Ouchies:

A hedgehog was mad at a bee
with spines as sharp as can be,
and rolled in a ball,
then started to bawl
when it was stung right on its knee.

Fast Food:

There once was a very young chick
that gave a corndog a lick.
But it got all flustered
because of the mustard,
and ended up dropping the stick.

Riddle:

I can barely hear any sound
and like digging underground.
Yet I have a small snoot
and will chew any root.
What critter am I?

Oddity:

There once was a small tiny roach
that pulled a very large coach,
but often it would tire
against its desire.

Feeders:

Hamsters can often sound squeaky
but also they can seem sneaky.
Yet once out of bed,
and as they are fed,
that's when they get very cheeky.

Oddity:

A frog once got a ride
after its green chauffeur lied.
Because it looked yummy
and fit in its tummy,
it never would see the other side.

Hoarders:

Never go blaming your spouse
if something gets lost in the house,
as it may seem unclear
when things disappear.
Instead go try asking this mouse.

Trainers:

There once was a funny kangaroo
who didn't like living in a zoo,
so he kicked his bad trainer,
and did a half gainer,
then punched while using Kung Fu.

Danger:

Aardvarks can seem kind of cute,
until you get smacked by their snoot.

Hiders:

Nobody likes seeing a rat
and many will tell it to scat,
yet if it can hide
down your backside,
it may bite you where you last sat.

Diggers:

There once was an angry old mole
whose back was too big for a hole,
so he screamed at his son
to widen him one
before he comes back from a stroll.

Riddle:

If you count all my toes
but don't see a nose,
it adds up to eight
and in seawater I wait.
What critter am I?

Snackers:

A lion that loved to relax
would sit back eating his snacks.
But it cost him so much
he charged it all up
using credit cards drawn to the max.

Night Owls:

Bats often fly out at night
while trying to stay out of sight.
But if one lands
and shows you its glands,
you just might die of a fright.

Readers:

A penguin once bet a dollar
that she'd out-fish a trawler.
So she sat in a nook
to learn from a book,
and now she's become a scholar.

Riddle:

I am like a green bean
with a bite that is mean,
and my tail can tattle
when it will rattle.
What critter am I?

Runners:

There once was a very fast horse
that tripped while running a course.
The jockey that led
got kicked in the head.
It neighed and showed no remorse.

Question:

Have you ever seen a young gnu
that really loves to chew?
It grazes all day
and nibbles away
until its face turns almost blue.

Polluters:

What's with the trash
that makes a big splash,
beyond the breakwater
where seagulls totter
while hunting for their stash?

Riddle:

I look like a crook
with hands like a cook,
and can scrounge at night
by your campsite.
What critter am I?

Oddity:

Have you ever gazed in the sky
and seen something up high,
that's big like a whale
with a curly cue tail?

Final Riddle:

I want to go on living
even way past Thanksgiving,
and my voice has a wobble
with every new gobble.
What critter am I?

Riddle Answers:
Page 9. Elephant 19. Whale Shark 33. Cheetah
41. Giraffe 59. Tortoise 69. Gopher 87. Octopus
95. Rattlesnake 103. Raccoon 107. Turkey

www.ingramcontent.com/pod-product-compliance
Lightning Source LLC
Chambersburg PA
CBHW021956090426
42811CB00001B/46